Ready to Preach

Ready to Use Sermons and Worship Resources

Paul Gonzalez

authorHOUSE®

AuthorHouse™
1663 Liberty Drive
Bloomington, IN 47403
www.authorhouse.com
Phone: 1-800-839-8640

Published by AuthorHouse 3/1/2012

ISBN: 978-1-4685-4307-0 (sc)
ISBN: 978-1-4685-4308-7 (e)

Library of Congress Control Number: 2012900719

"The Lord thy God in the midst of thee is mighty: He will save, He will rejoice over thee with joy: He will rest in His love, He will joy over thee with singing." - Zephaniah 3: 17

WELCOME:

On this third Sunday of Advent, we sincerely welcome each and every one of you who have come to worship our Lord Jesus Christ. May the Lord bless you with His grace, refresh your mind, renew your spirit, and fill you with joy through this service.

INVOCATION:

Dear Heavenly Father of our Lord Jesus Christ, You have sent Your Son to live among us. Receive our songs of praise as we worship You this day. Fill our hearts with hope, peace, and joy that we may declare Your salvation. In Jesus' name, Amen.

OFFERING PRAYER:

Dear Lord Jesus, we come before You offering these tithes that You have so abundantly blessed into our lives. Like Mary and Joseph, we often worry about how life is going. But, we forget that You are already ahead of us. Accept what we have given this day, use it for Your Kingdom and Your glory, to help others in need. Bless us with joy in our lives to enjoy this third week of advent. In Jesus' name, Amen.

PRAYER FOR THE FAMILY OF GOD:

Our Father which art in Heaven, we come in Jesus' name before Your beautiful presence. As we face so many problems in this season of Advent, we worry about so many things. You remind us through Your precious word that you told the kings, prophets, and Israel that if they wanted a sign, all they had to do was to knock and it would be opened, to ask and they would receive, but they had to seek for it. At this moment we ask, seek, and knock, dear Lord. We give You thanks for hearing us and answering us that we may joyously accept Your answer and follow that path that leads us to everlasting joy. Lord, there are so many people asking about Your guidance. Teach us and help us to tell them of Your joy, love, and grace, and Your concern for us. Lead us to eternal life. In Jesus' name, Amen.

BENEDICTION:

O Lord, send us forth into the third week of Advent, seeking Your signs. Send us forth with Your hope, peace, and joy. Send us forth as Your people to experience Your birth into our lives this Christmas. Amen!

SUGGESTED HYMNS:

"Joy to the World"
"Hark, the Herald Angels Sing"
"Rejoice in the Lord Always"
"Spirit Song"
"He Keeps Me Singing"

SERMON #1: THE JOY OF THE LORD

Isaiah 51:4-11, Luke2:8-20
Advent

Today, we celebrate the third week of Advent as we move towards Christmas. We will continue, in our sermon, by looking at the meaning of the candle we lit, today. The first candle represents peace, the second candle stands for the preparation of hope, and the third one for joy. Christmas carols and decorations are filled with joy during this time of the year, but we have to take a closer look at what that really means. It is more than happiness. Do you know that the most beautiful and precious things are supposed to be felt with the heart? Just like music, it is felt with the heart.

The wife of a poor merchant died, leaving her husband with five children, ranging from age six to fifteen years. The older children did many of the household chores: cooking, cleaning, and helping the younger children. When the father came home, at night, he always brought a bag of groceries for the next day. After he set the bag on the table, he gave each of his children a hug. Before they ate, the father read a few Scriptures and the family prayed. Many nights, before bed, the children begged their father to sing with them. He often played his guitar and sang folk songs.

The first Christmas, after his wife died, the father said to his children, "This year, there is not enough money to buy presents. Instead, we will all draw names, and you will make a present for one of your brothers or sisters. My gift to you will be a fine Christmas meal and a special song that I am writing. We will learn it, in the weeks before Christmas, and sing it in church on Christmas Eve." True to his word, the father wrote a beautiful song of joy for the children, and began to teach the song to them, three weeks before the Nativity. The children loved the song so much; they sang it loud with joy.

It so happened that a rich man, who hated music and Christmas, lived right above the family. Night after night, he listened to the children rehearsing the new Christmas song. It irritated him so much that he planned to silence the singing. Several days before Christmas, he knocked on the door. "I have come to make you an offer," he said to the father who listened carefully with his children standing right behind him. "I will give you one hundred gold coins if you promise not to sing for three months."

The father looked at his children and said, "That's more money than I can make in two years! We will be able to buy presents for everyone in the family." The children applauded and cheered joyfully, as the father accepted the money on the rich man's terms. That night, they began to plan silently how they would spend the money.

Over the next few evenings, they ate, and sat quietly, reading and thinking. On the fourth night, one of the children said, "I would rather have music than presents. This silence isn't worth it." One by one, the children agreed.

So, the father walked into the bedroom, grabbed the money bag, and climbed upstairs to return the money to its owner. He told the man, "We have discovered there is something more important than money. I am sorry that our singing bothers you, but it fills us with joy. Our family cannot imagine Christmas, or life, without the joy of music."

When the father returned to his children, he said, "We will learn to sing with greater feelings and softer voices. In our joy, we do not want to disturb our neighbor. Okay?"

The oldest child spoke out for all, "The children of the Lord shall return, and come with singing unto God, and everlasting joy shall be with us. We shall obtain gladness and joy, and sorrow and mourning shall flee away."

The father and the children did not have much material things, but they had joy through their music and hope – hope in Jesus Christ.

With Christmas just a couple of weeks away, we don't need a calendar to remind us. There is not a house or a store in town that does not have Christmas decorations. To Christians, that means Jesus is coming with His glory, not Santa Claus with his reindeers. We celebrate His coming for three reasons:

First, Christmas is the fulfilling of God's prophecies from the Old Testament. A prophecy is a statement, made by someone proclaiming a message from God, predicting an event in advance of its occurrence. Six hundred ninety seven years before Christ was born, the Prophet Micah accurately named the small village of Bethlehem as the place where the Messiah was to be born. Seven hundred fifty years before Christ, Isaiah prophesied, "Therefore, the Lord Himself will give you a sign. Behold, the virgin shall conceive and bear a Son, and shall call His name Emmanuel (God with us!)." And it happened just as Isaiah prophesied.

In the second chapter of Luke we read, "The angel of the Lord appeared unto the shepherds and said, 'Behold, I bring unto you good news of great joy. For unto you a Savior has been born today, in the city of David, in Bethlehem, Christ the Lord!' And it came to pass, that when the angels were gone from their sight into heaven they said, 'Let us go and see this thing which came to pass, which the Lord hath made known unto us.' And they came rapidly and found Mary, and Joseph, and the babe lying in a manger."

And ever since, for two thousand and eleven years, this story has been told. It is an everlasting story and Jesus is the everlasting One. Christmas fulfills our joy and all the prophecy proclamations. But, that's not all! There's still more to this. Christ was born fulfilling the prophecy. But now, He has to walk through His life, here on earth, and fulfill the rest of the prophecies.

Second, Jesus proclaims the fulfillment of His prophecy. There are over three hundred prophecies concerning the Messiah. Six hundred and five years before Christ, the Prophet Daniel prophesied that the Messiah would begin His ministry here on earth: to restore and rebuild this earth called Jerusalem. This was supposed to be the New Jerusalem. But, some would rather serve sin than Jesus. Jesus said, in Matthew 23:27, "O Jerusalem, Jerusalem, you who kill the prophets and stone those who were sent to you, how often have I longed to gather your children together, as a hen gathers her chicks under her wings, but you are not willing."

Four hundred years before Christ, crucifixion was invented for capital punishment. And it was before this, David prophesied in Psalm 22:1, "My God, My God, why hast Thou forsaken me?" David also prophesied, "He keepeth all His bones, and not one of them is broken." (Psalm 34:20) This was a custom of the crucifixion to make death sure.

Then Zechariah (11:12, 13) prophesies the Messiah will be betrayed, for thirty pieces of silver, and the money will be used to buy a burial ground. Again, five hundred eighty years before Christ, Zechariah (12:10) prophesied "They shall look upon me, whom they have pierced, and they shall mourn. In that day, there shall be a great mourning in Jerusalem."

This is the Savior we celebrate at Christmas in the twenty first century! "For unto us a child is born, Christ the Lord!"

Third, we celebrate because it proclaims the purpose of the birth of Jesus Christ. For more than forty generations, Jesus has saved millions of people, both young and old alike. And we rejoice because of this! This Christmas, let us remember the virgin birth, the crowded inn in Bethlehem, the shepherds watching their flocks by night, the wise men traveling from countries afar as they follow the star in the East, the babe Jesus wrapped in swaddling clothes and lying in a manger. And through all of this meditation and celebration, let us not forget that Jesus Christ came to give His life for many and to pay the ultimate price, so that we might have eternal life.

The story of Jesus is beautiful, and it is absolutely true!

For some, Christmas begins and ends in Bethlehem. For some, they ignore Calvary at Christmas time, and it never satisfies them spiritually. This is why we come to church – to be strengthened and satisfied spiritually. Christmas is all about rejoicing in the Lord always! The secret of the stable, and of a joyful life, still lies where the prophets found it, in the assurance that God is with us, manifesting His name Emmanuel – God is with us. He is resting above us and rejoicing over us, receiving our praises unto Him! If our love grabs hold of His love, and His joy finds its way into our hearts, it will remain there alive. It is alive, church, "so that our joy may be full!" Even though there is still the fear of stumbling, Jesus is there, guarding us and guiding us, until He sets us free – free at last – "in the presence of His glory with exceeding joy." (Jude 1:24)

Let's get it right, this year. Christmas is coming and our celebration is about the coming of the Lord, not as a baby, but as our Savior! He is telling us, "Go ye therefore and share with all people." Tell your neighbor, "God is talking to you." Yes, God is talking to you and to me. So, rejoice always in the Lord, and again, I say, "Rejoice, church!" Amen!

WORSHIP PLANNING HELPS #2

> "Therefore be ready: for in such an hour as you think not, the Son of Man comes."
> – Matthew 24:44

WELCOME:

We welcome to this second Sunday in Advent, all who have joined with us in waiting for the coming of our Lord Jesus Christ. May this time of worship be uplifting to all.

INVOCATION:

O Lord, as we move through this season of Advent, renew our vision of the task You came to place before us as Your church. Touch again our hearts with hope and make us ready to serve You and anticipate Your return. Amen.

CALL TO WORSHIP:

L: Let us sing and celebrate for God has brought salvation to us all.
C: The salvation promised to the most ancient of Israel.
L: And salvation for those of every nation and of every tribe.
C: Great is the God of Israel who sent us a Savior for all mankind!
ALL: Blessed be the name of the Lord!

OFFERING PRAYER:

Dear Lord, in Jesus' name, we bring these tithes and offerings unto Thee. We ask for Your blessing upon us. We know You are an amazing God who can take what we have given and produce amazing fruit. In Jesus who is our hope, we pray. Amen.

PRAYER FOR THE FAMILY OF GOD

Dear Lord,

As we draw closer to the celebration of Your birth at Christmas, we find the carols of the season inspiring us to rejoice in praising You. In spite of the problems through this holy season, we still sense Your spirit in our midst. As the prophet Isaiah reminds us, the most deserted places can blossom and the feelings that are polluted with greed and selfishness can suddenly bloom in Your presence. May we work together like the prophets of old who never quit, but brought honor to You. May we work hard like the farmers who till the soil and plant the seeds, who tend their plants, and wait in patience, praying for praise to take over the season. We ask for the right questions so we can take the right direction. John wanted to know if You were the right one or if the people should wait for someone else. Many people still ask their own questions. Use us to answer them by being examples through our works and actions. You have given us the job to change materialism to praise and greed to a desire for Your kingdom. You have given us the patience to journey through this season leading people to Your kingdom through the highway called the Holy Road that leads to heaven and is now open to us. Thank You for the grace of Your beloved Son as we walk through this season, serving You. Amen.

SUGGESTED HYMNS:

"O Come, All Ye Faithful"
"Solid Rock"
"In the Presence of Jehovah"
"Angels We Have Heard on High"
"Go, Tell It on the Mountain"

BENEDICTION:

Go forth and make your hearts ready for the coming of the Lord. Rejoice in His nearness and proclaim the message of salvation to those around you. Be blessed and be a blessing to all who cross your path that Jesus might be praised. Amen.

SERMON #2: ARE YOU READY?

Psalm 2, Isaiah 9:2-7, Mark 1:1-8
Advent

The mother took the Christmas boxes down from the attic. Then, she and her three year old started putting up the Christmas tree. She took the box of the nativity scene, and told the boy to give her one piece at a time. As he unwrapped each piece, he said, "Here's a camel. Here's a king. Here's a cow. Here's a donkey. Here's baby Jesus sitting in His car seat." Well, it is not a car seat, but a manger. We all love to see the nativity scene of baby Jesus lying in a manger with Mary and Joseph looking over the baby Jesus while wise men, camels, cattle, sheep, a donkey, and a little drummer boy gaze in wonder.

But, there's one person missing. Have you ever seen a nativity scene with John the Baptist in it? He would be this hairy, unkempt, wild looking young man. You know how the hair style is today. They just shake their hair and put on hair spray. Well, I haven't seen a nativity scene with John the Baptist in it.

But, on the second week of Advent, we always encounter him sounding his message out to the wilderness. "Prepare ye the way of the Lord." The gospels give us a short outline of John's life. The gospels tell us that John was Jesus' second cousin and that John, too, was a miraculous birth. His parents were quite elderly when he was born. The Scriptures say that Gabriel, an angel of God, appeared to a priest named Zachariah who would be John's father. Zachariah was in the temple performing his duties when he had a visit from Gabriel who gave him a message to prepare himself because he and Elizabeth were going to have a son, even though she was far past the normal child bearing age. Zachariah became speechless at this announcement. He didn't believe this great news. So, the angel told Zachariah, "Because you did not believe my message, you shall be mute until the child is born. Then, you shall call his name John, and you shall receive your voice back."

Zachariah and Elizabeth were from the priesthood lineage. This means they were church people, no different than you and me. They were spiritually alive enough for Zachariah to see the angel of God and for Elizabeth to receive the blessing.

When Elizabeth was six months pregnant, her cousin Mary came to visit her and shared with Elizabeth the miraculous news of her pregnancy. When they were witnessing about each of their experiences with the angel Gabriel, the Holy Spirit came upon them and both babies leaped for joy in their wombs. They both had great testimonies to share. This is what happens, church, when we witness to other people about what the Lord has done for us. But, don't worry; each one of us has a different gift through which we feel the presence of the Lord in us.

Well, John grew up and became a preacher of justice and righteousness who called people to a baptism of repentance. And guess who came to be baptized? His cousin Jesus! Jesus was just getting ready to start His ministry. Matthew, Luke, and John tell us that John did not want to baptize Jesus. Instead, he said, "I need to be baptized by You." But, Jesus told Him that the Scriptures needed to be fulfilled. So, John agreed to baptize Jesus. (Matthew 3:13)

The Scriptures are very clear about John's part in the drama of the nativity. John was to prepare the way for the Lord; to turn the hearts of the fathers and mothers to their children and the disobedient to the righteousness of God. Church, it is here! The same thing is happening right before our eyes. Some parents are murdering their own children. It is all over this world. And now, the coming of the Lord is next. Church, we are so close to the end. I can imagine how John was using the anointing of Elijah; he had a double portion of the spirit and power of God. He was revealing Revelation 11, fulfilling Scriptures from the Old to the New Testament. Matthew 11:10-15 says, "For this is He of whom it is written." Remember Malachi? "Behold, I send my witness before thy face, which shall prepare the way before thee! There has not been born a greater than John the Baptist. From the days of John until now, the kingdom of heaven suffers violence and violence taketh it by force. He that has ears to hear, let him hear what the spirit saith to the church." All the Old Testament law and prophets prophesied until this came to pass. If you will, John was Elijah who was prophesied to come! I believe this was one of the two witnesses in Revelation 11, because it took only one witness to prepare the way of the Lord. And I believe that the next witness is already here, preparing his ministry for the second coming of the Lord! Are you ready?

The four gospels have a very different way of introducing the story about Jesus. The Savior was born in Bethlehem, but the world still waits for Him. That is the meaning of Advent. Advent is the celebration of what has been and what is yet to come. The Savior of the world came to us in the Babe of Bethlehem, but this was just the beginning of God's redeeming work. It is so easy to relax and to focus on the beauty and joy of Christmas than it is to focus on the Advent season; especially when we are going through all these trials, battles, and storms of life as we await God's final victory over sin and suffering. This is what Christmas is all about; the season when all spiritual attention turns with hope to the second coming of Jesus Christ. And we do know that He is coming back! Amen, church?! Are you ready?

We may be celebrating His first coming in a few weeks, but it is His second coming that we are waiting for with hope. So, let me ask you, this morning, what are you watching on TV? Is it the morning news, the next American idol, or the soaps? Whatever it is, if Christ's return is not breaking the news or your program, they are in trouble! If the radio station, you are hearing, is not programming this, once in a while, then, they are in trouble! We do not want to be caught like an ostrich with his head in the sand or the surrey horse, staring straight ahead with blinders on. If anything is important, it is the coming of Jesus Christ. And how can we be sure that we will not miss Christ when He returns? Are you ready?

There are three simple things we need to do. The first thing; we need to be dedicated and committed. He bought this church with His blood on Calvary.. He is not returning for pew warmers or holiday church goers unless you have an excuse such as being sick or disabled. He is not coming back for a membership with no discipleship. He is coming back for all those who have accepted Him as Lord of lords and Savior. He is coming back for those who have repented for their sinful acts and are dedicated to serving Him always. He is coming back for those who worship Him in spirit and in truth; not Santa's celebration or party planning. This will not count as worship! Our commitment to worshiping and serving Him is forever and ever.

The second thing is to be alert! Do not be caught sleeping on the job. Be watchful for the changes that lead closer to the end of times. We won't hear radio stations programming the date and time of Christ's return. Some things we just have to do ourselves. We are called to be observant; to "watch therefore", and be attentive. If we don't pay attention, He will sneak up on us as a thief in the night and catch us unaware. Let us not be like the Pharisees and Scribes who Jesus rebuked for their ignorance, saying, "O you hypocrites! You are good at reading the weather, the signs of the skies, but you failed to read the signs of the times." We don't want to hear the Lord say this to us.

The third thing is to be ready. If we are the body of Christ, we should be geared up, organized, and equipped for Jesus' return. We should be ready to witness. We should read the Upper Room or another daily devotion that will get us ready for the day to share the good news with others. This s a good way of witnessing and reaching our family members who have not yet accepted Jesus. The hour is coming when it will be too late! Are you ready?

A couple from the United States went on a missionary trip to the former Soviet Republics. They were caring for children in an orphanage. Like any other children's ministry, they were just overwhelmed by the tragedy of so many children who had been abandoned. During the Advent season, the missionary couple was teaching the children about Christmas. They told them about Mary and Joseph, the shepherds, the wise men, and about the baby Jesus. They told the children all about the stable, the manger, and the star in the sky. They told them all about God's love for the world in the birth of Jesus. After teaching the Christmas story, on Christmas Eve, this couple invited the kids to draw some pictures of the manger scene. All of the pictures were wonderful, but one in particular caught their attention. It was drawn by a little boy name Misha. What made Misha's drawing distinctive was that there was not one, but two babies lying in the manger. "Misha, what a wonderful picture!" said the woman missionary. "But, who is the other baby in the manger with the baby Jesus?" Misha looked up with a lovely expression on his face. "The other baby is Misha," he said with a smile. "Oh? How is it that you added yourself to the manger scene?" she asked. Misha said, "When I was drawing the picture of baby Jesus, Jesus looked at me and asked, "Misha, where is your family?" I said to Jesus, "I have no family." Then, Jesus said to me, "Misha, where is your home?" And I said to Jesus, "I have no home." And Jesus said to me, "Misha, you can come and be in my family and live in my home." "So, Misha went to lie down with baby Jesus," Misha concluded. This is a lovely story, and we are so thankful for missionaries who tell people like Misha in the Soviet Union, about Jesus.

But, lots of people out there in the world are still waiting for a Savior. You will find them in the neighborhood, town, or city. We will find them in our own community. But, the Savior has come and people who have not received Jesus in their hearts are lost and condemned forever.

Christ will return, and truly, the day will come when everybody will see the One who saw our sin and saved us; the One who realized our guilt and pardoned us; the One who knew our despair and redeemed us! Will you be found alert? Will you be found with boldness and joyful anticipation? Will you be found watching with salvation? Will you be ready for the journey? Church, are you ready? Say it with me: "I am ready!" Amen!

WORSHIP PLANNING HELPS #3

"My sheep hear My voice and they follow Me." – John 10:27

WELCOME:

God wants a cheerful and thankful heart when we come to worship Him. Let this time of worship be spent in gratitude for God's goodness toward us. So, with joyful hearts, let us praise the Lord!

INVOCATION:

Heavenly Father,
You sent Your Son, Jesus, to be our Lord and Savior. We acknowledge Him as King of kings and Lord of lords, and bow in worship to bring glory and honor to His holy name. Amen.

CALL TO WORSHIP:

L: Grace unto you and peace from God who was and who is and who is to come.
C: And from Jesus Christ, the faithful witness, ruler above all rulers of the earth.
L: In love, Jesus Christ suffered death to free us from our sins.
C: Making all who confess Christ a nation of priests set aside for God's service.
ALL: To Jesus Christ be glory and power forever and ever! Amen.

OFFERING PRAYER:

O Lord,
In Jesus' precious name, we come before Thee. It is our desire to give thanks unto Thee and to present these tithes as our gift unto Thee. Bless them and use them that others may know Your goodness and grace. Share Your joy and blessings with us, O Lord, in Your abundant life. Amen!

PRAYER FOR THE FAMILY OF GOD

Dear Heavenly Father,
In Jesus' precious name, we come humbly before Your beautiful glory. We are Your children. We love to be in Your care and comfort. We know that You want the best for us. Yet, we stumble, sometimes, and come like willful children unto Thee. Have Your authority in our lives and remain steadfast; forgiving and calling us back to Your righteousness. Have Your eyes set upon us for You are the only way we can be strengthened and have a relationship with You. Through Your Holy Spirit, You bless us with happiness, joy, and peace. Holy, holy, holy are You. For heaven and earth are filled with Your glory. Open our eyes to see Your glory. Open our ears to hear Your voice. Open our mouths to proclaim our testimonies. Open our hands to share Your love. Guide our feet to the places where You would have us serve. Here we are, use us for Your glory. Amen.

Paul Gonzalez

SUGGESTED HYMNS:
"All Hail the Power of Jesus' Name"
"There's Something About That Name"
"Jesus is Lord of All"
"Lord, Prepare Me"
"I Know Whom I Have Believed"

BENEDICTION:
Go forth in the fruit of the Spirit and in the grace of Jesus Christ and in the love of God. Through His Holy Spirit, may God grant you, this week, your petitions and show You His way, His truth, and His life! Be blessed. Amen.

SERMON #3: WHO DO YOU THINK YOU ARE?

John 10:22-27
Advent

In a particular Peanuts comic scene, Snoopy is sitting in the doorway of his dog house, shivering and cold, during a winter storm. You can see that it is after Thanksgiving, because they are just putting the Christmas decorations on the dog house. Charlie Brown and Lucy are walking by, all bundled up in their warm coats. They give Snoopy a greeting. "Be of good cheer, Snoopy!" Charlie Brown says. "Yes, be of good cheer!" Lucy replies. And they keep walking by as Snoopy sits there with chattering teeth. Snoopy says, "Won't you please share a blanket rather than a farewell greeting?"

That's how the Jews felt as they were complaining when Jesus was preaching the Word of God with a compassionate heart. Instead, they would respond, "Who do you think you are? If you really are the Messiah, why aren't you a king? Don't confront us with your parables and your mysteries. Don't try to take away our Torah Law Moses gave to us." Isn't it ironic, that in those days, these same people had heard Jesus preaching the truth with power and performing miracles right before their eyes. The problem was not that Jesus was refusing to proclaim His deity, but the problem was the Jews and their beliefs. The Jews were only pretending not to understand. They understood it, all right, but they refused to believe it. They hardened their hearts towards the Word of God.

Let me ask this morning, what did the Jews believe about Jesus? In John, chapter seven, some believed Jesus was a good man. "For neither did His brethren believe in Him." (7:5) They believed He was a just man. Contrary to what some denominations believe, Jesus never called God "Jehovah" and the Mormons never call God "Jesus". They believe they will be more than man. Hear the name: "more than man". They believe they will be a god. They eliminate Jesus as one of the Trinity: Father, Son, and Holy Spirit; the three in one. I think of a gum. It's juicy, fruity, and chewy. But, if you don't chew it, it's not gum.

Some Jews, Pharisees, and Scribes looked at Jesus as a deceiver, a man who was leading people away from their religion. Others thought Jesus was just a man who was not important enough to be worth the risk of supporting Him and defending Him. The Pharisees, Scribes, and Jews would not accept His high authority as "The Messiah". They would huddle and ask one another, "How does this man know so much? What credentials does He have to be a teacher? Who is He claiming to be? He's the son of Joseph, the carpenter by trade. They looked at Jesus, and they yelled out, "Who do you think you are?" All this mixed bag of Jews told Jesus, "Prove to us you are the Messiah!" They were all in agreement with this.

It is no different than now days. Those who doubt the deity of Jesus still say, "Why should I believe in Him? He hasn't done anything for me, lately." Some forget the fact that He just brought them out of a tough situation, last week or last month. Some say, "What proof do we have that He was sent by God? Prove to us!" Why do some people have a problem accepting Jesus for who He is? He was given the throne of the Father, and sits at the right hand of God. Some would rather follow a good man than Jesus. Some would rather follow an athlete than Jesus. Some would rather follow hollywood stars than Jesus. Some would rather believe a non-Christian than a believer in Jesus. What does Jesus have to do in order to win our love and devotion?

Just as your spouse won you over with flowers and a box of candy or your boss won you over with a raise or your neighbor won you over with a home cooked, delicious turkey plate, or your mother-in-law won you over when she babysat the kids, God is trying to win us over. That's why He sent His only begotten Son, Jesus, to die on the cross for you and me.

Yet, people still question His motivation and His deity? "Who do you think you are, Jesus?" Is this a tough question? The Jews asked, "How long are you going to make us doubt? Why are you playing church? Why are you trying to puzzle us?" But, Jesus quickly responded, "I have done no such thing. I told you who I am." In John 6:38, Jesus admitted, "I am sent by God, and I came down from heaven, to do my Father's will." John 7:29: "I know the Father, for I am from Him, and He hath sent me, to do His will." John 8:28: "When you shall lift up the Son of Man, then shall you know, that I Am that I Am, and I do nothing of Myself, but as my Father has taught Me, I speak of those things." Then, Jesus challenged those who claimed to know the Father; "If God were your Father, then, you would love Me, for I proceed forth from the Father. I didn't choose to come, but He sent Me, and so, I must do the works of Him who sent Me, while it is daylight, for I have nothing to hide."

There was nothing secret about Jesus. He did more than just talk about who He was. If proof was what they wanted, they should have had enough with the miracles. On the first day of His earthly ministry, hundreds witnessed the heavens opening and hearing a voice saying, "This is My beloved Son, hear Him." At the wedding in Cana, they witnessed the water turned into the best wine. Then, there was the miracle healing of the fever stricken body of the son of a nobleman who looked for Jesus until he found Him and asked Him to come and heal his son. Jesus answered, "Except you see signs and wonders you believe not." And he replied, "Please, Sir, come before my son dies." Jesus said, "Go thy way, thy son lives." (John 4:46) And remember the miracle at the pool in Bethesda, the house of mercy, where Jesus healed a man who had been crippled for thirty eight years while waiting for the stirring of the water? Jesus asked him, "Will thou be made whole?" "Sir, I can't." "Rise, take up thy bed and walk." (John 5:1) There was the cleansing of a demonic man in the synagogue. There was the healing of Peter's sick mother-in-law who had a terrible headache, and the healing of the multitude that followed and showed up for the same reason. (Matthew 8:14) A healing took place for the paralytic man who was lowered from Paul's roof top to be in the presence of Jesus. There was the cleansing of a man who had leprosy. (Matthew 8:2) There was the healing of the man with the withered hand. There was the miracle of the centurion's servant, and the miracle of the widow's dead son who was raised to life.

The most powerful emotion in all of these people was their response to the Lord. All of these thirty six miracles that Jesus performed are written so that we might believe in Him. But, the response from the Jews was, "Who do you think you are?"

No wonder Jesus said, "You've seen the miracles I have done in my Father's power, and yet, you say, 'Who do you think you are? Prove to us!' You are not my sheep! The sheep know the shepherd's voice, do they not?"

In the New Testament, we read about Jesus Christ. His word is recorded just for us. There are three ways Jesus proved His deity. First, He did the will of the Father. He talked the talk and He walked the walk. Jesus said if a person obeys His Father, then he belongs to His Father. He wasn't talking about storing biblical knowledge to impress friends and neighbors. He wasn't playing a role on Sunday or Wednesday. He talked about who God is. Jesus certified His deity when He obeyed His Father and refused to come down from heaven to judge the world. He followed God's divine plan of redemption all the way to the cross with love.

Secondly, Jesus' deity was performed. He never spoke for His glory; He spoke about His Father's glory. He claimed to be the truth, sent from His Father. He did not represent the Father, and then, accept the credit for Himself. He was going to sit down on the throne of His Father to represent the New Testament, and the Father sat down on the Old Testament throne to represent the Old Testament.

Thirdly, we can use the law and tell if Jesus is true. Anyone can follow the law and know if he is keeping it. Jesus never broke the law. He kept the law of His Father, not the law of men because it was doctrines of men, not of God. (I John 4:1) Paul warns us about false doctrines of men.

But, your relationship with Jesus is a personal decision. You either believe or not. Jesus has already done all He has been allowed to do, to convince us, that He is Lord of lords. We can be like the religious Pharisees, Jews, Scribes and keep on saying, "Who do you think you are?" Or, we can be like sheep who know the voice of their Shepherd when He calls us. I know Him by His bounty and beauty, and you know Him by His blessings and boldness. I know Him by His promises and perfection; you know Him by His majesty and mercy. I know Him by His lowliness and loveliness; you know Him by His truth and trust. I know Him by His justice and joy; you know Him by His kingdom and kindness. We know Him by our service and our relationship with Him. We don't have to say, "Who do you think you are?' We can say together, "I know in Whom I have believed – in Jesus Christ and to God be all the glory! Amen.

"Let us come before His presence with thanksgiving." – Psalm 95:2

WELCOME:

Welcome! Let's express our gratitude to God on this Sunday before Thanksgiving. We rejoice in God's presence. Let us joyfully praise God through prayer, song, and reflection on His word.

INVOCATION:

O God, our Father,
We bow before You with grateful hearts for Your bountiful goodness to us. You have blessed us, in so many ways, we cannot begin to count them. Most of all, we thank You for the gift of Your Son, Jesus Christ. His life, His death, His resurrection, and His ascension have shown us the way to eternal life with You. With hearts filled with hope, joy, and thankfulness, we praise Your holy name. Amen.

CALL TO WORSHIP:

L: Shout for joy to the Lord, all the earth!
C: Worship the Lord with gladness; come before Him with joyful songs.
L: Know that the Lord is God. It is He who made us, and we are His; we are His people, the sheep of His pasture.
C: Enter His gates with thanksgiving; and His courts with praise; give thanks to Him and praise His name.
ALL: For the Lord is good and His love endures forever; His faithfulness continues through all generations.

OFFERING PRAYER:

In Jesus' precious name, O God, You provide blessings and riches from Your kingdom. We thank You and offer unto Thee, with joy, these tithes in honor of Your beloved Son, Jesus. Bless these gifts for Your kingdom work. Bless those who gave with a cheerful heart. Amen.

PRAYER FOR THE FAMILY OF GOD

Dear Heavenly Father,
Thank You for this day and Your presence with us as we remember the wonders that You have done and the blessings and protection You have given for the purpose of Your kingdom. It is good to remember the great needs and sufferings of those we know and Your faithfulness in our lives. We depend on that faithfulness, even today, as we face the coming week. We can depend on Your precious word, and we are able to do far more than we ask or think. We thank You for our family and we thank You, Jesus, for calling us by our name and reminding us that each given day is for thanksgiving because of You. Amen.

SUGGESTED HYMNS:
"I Will Enter His Gates"
"Great Is Thy Faithfulness"
"Blessed Assurance"
"Spirit of the Living God"
"Give Thanks"
"Count Your Blessings"

BENEDICTION:
May the Lord bless you and keep you; may He make His face and spirit to shine upon you, and be gracious to you; may He lift you up and give you a smile, and bless you with His fruit of love, joy, peace, happiness, goodness, faith, and strength this coming week. In Jesus' name. Amen.

SERMON #4: HAPPY THANKSGIVING!

Psalm 100; Philippians 4:1-9

Today, I took the bus, and I sat across from a nice lady with brownish hair. I envied her. She seemed so nice and spirit filled. Oh, how I wished, I was like that. When the bus stopped, she rose to leave, but as she passed by, she smiled, and said, "Hi!" I saw her hobble down the aisle; she had one foot and wore a crutch. I said, "Oh, God, forgive me when I complain. I have two feet and the whole world is mine. Thank you, Lord."

When I got off the bus, I stopped to buy some sweets at the store. The young man who attended me had such charm. He seemed so calm and full of good cheer. His manner was so kind and warm. I said, "It's nice to visit with you. Such courtesy I seldom find." He said, "Thank you, sir." As he turned to give me my change, he felt for my hands. Then, I knew that he was blind. "Oh, God, forgive me when I whine. I have two eyes and the world is mine. Thank you, Lord."

Then, walking down the street, I saw a child poorly dressed. As he stood and watched the other kids play, it seemed he knew not what to say. I stopped for a moment and I asked him, "Why don't you join the others?" He paid no attention and kept looking ahead without a word. Then, I knew he could not hear; he was deaf. And I said, "Oh, Lord, forgive me, for I have two ears and the world is mine.

Thank you, Lord. I have two feet to take me where I would go; with eyes to see the sunset glow; with ears to hear what I would know. I am so blessed, dear Lord. Please forgive me when I moan, for the world is mine. Thank you, Lord, for this life of mine."

Thanksgiving is a unique holiday in the United States. It all began with a Christian purpose. In Psalm 100, the word 'praise' refers to thanksgiving. This is a song that the Israelites would sing to God when He would rescue them out of their troubles. Their belief came out of the Torah, their sacred writings, and by hearing the word of God. Now, we have the B-I-B-L-E. What does that spell? The word of God says, "That as many as received Jesus, to them gave He the power to become the children of God." (John 1:12)

When the pioneer settlers gathered with the Indians on that famous day, it was for the purpose of thanking God for their blessings. Today, we would hardly recognize this day in many homes. Some people call it, "Gobble Day." while others don't even celebrate it as a day of thanksgiving unto God. It is known, that on this holiday, church services are one of the emptiest places in the United States. People put too much emphasis on who is going to host this holiday. Some people spend days planning the dinner. Oh, don't forget the snacks for the football game, either. Some can't even find a resemblance between the first Thanksgiving and the one we will be celebrating. Sometimes, I think there are some unthankful people in this nation. And some don't even train their children to say "Thank you"; much less thank God for His goodness. We should all be thankful in our lives if we expect blessings to continue flowing from the throne of Jesus. Hebrews 4:16 says, "Let us come boldly before the throne of Jesus that we may obtain mercy, and find grace to help in time of need." Psalm 100 tells us to "make a joyful noise to the Lord." In the Hebrew translation, it says, "to shout in triumph and to applaud to Jeshua," which is Jesus. So, let's not be too reserved in our worship. It's time to use what we have reserved in church! Amen? Amen!

There's a foundational principle in thanksgiving; it is to believe that it belongs to God. In giving thanks, He demonstrates His power to us. We will receive His joy and peace and our blessings, too, when we believe. "All ye people" means it is for everyone to join in! In Psalm 100, David says, we should "serve the Lord with gladness." The word 'serve' means to evangelize and thank God, too. We will be rewarded for this, here on earth and in heaven. So, let's start thanking God for our family daily. Cast those bad habits away from them in Jesus' name if you want to see God's power in your loved ones.

David says, "Make a joyful noise unto the Lord, all ye lands." Take advantage of this first day of the week. It belongs to God. We know that every first thing belongs to God. But, when we come to worship on Sundays, God is here on His throne and Jesus is on the Father's right side – not my right side or your right side!

When an angel appeared to me, He gave me this message: "You have tears to share the gospel with. We don't up here. So, use them and give them the gospel message." So, today is the opportunity that we have to praise the Father and the Son and the Holy Spirit. This is not an option if we truly are Christians. Our hearts should start getting ready when we jump out of bed on Sunday mornings; even better, when our feet are walking in the church of God with thanksgiving in our hearts. No matter how hard it is!

It's like Bob and Joe who were walking home and decided to make a short cut through a fenced field. Halfway through, they spotted a black bull. Instantly, they ran towards the nearest fence, as fast as their feet could take them. The storming bull followed in hot pursuit, and it looked like they weren't going to make it. Terrified, Joe shouted to Bob, "Start praying, Bob! We're in for it!" As the bull was approaching even closer, Joe yelled out, "Pray, Bob, pray!" "I can't," answered Bob, "I've never made a public prayer before in my life." "Please, you must!" shouted Joe. "Okay," said Bob, "I'll say the only prayer I know. It's the one my father would always repeat at the table: 'O Lord, for what we are about to receive, make us truly thankful.'"

Our voices will catch up with our hearts and they will get louder in praise and adoration and they will start producing fruit out of us when we worship God in giving thanks. Music is an emotional response to the blessings of God. God designed it to be for Him; and people want to change it for the world and for their own purpose. What I am saying is that listening to Christian music is helpful to worship God in church. But, some listen to worldly music, and then, they have a hard time separating the two in their minds. Singing, if it is done for a good purpose, gives Jesus the glory. It was given to us from the beginning of time, but, Lucifer stole it from us to destroy the minds of people.

Ignorance destroys the blessings and that reduces the thanksgiving. Guilt is a terrible motivation for giving thanks. The few blessings people receive, they are not even aware of them. David says, in Psalm 100:3, "He has made us, not we ourselves." How can God's creation turn away and refuse His ways? How can we refuse to acknowledge God as our creator? Thanksgiving was made to celebrate with the family God has joined together. "We are His people and the sheep of His pasture." We are adopted into His family and heirs of His salvation and of His kingdom through His grace. Romans 8:16 states, "His spirit bears witness with our spirit, that we are the children of God." Jesus says, "I am the good Shepherd and I lay down my life for you." Should we not be thankful that God takes such good care of us? David says, in Psalm 104, "Enter into His gates with thanksgiving and into His courts with praise, and be thankful unto Him and bless His name."

My three points are these: We worship God from public praise to personal praise to privileged praise, blessing His name. First, in public praise, we rejoice when others invite us to church worship. In Psalm 122:1, David says, "I was glad when they said unto me; let us go unto the house of the Lord." Psalm 92:13 declares, "Those that be planted in the church of the Lord will flourish in the courts of our God." We want others to see that we are thankful unto God for His blessings.

Second, personal praise comes out of our hearts in adoration unto God. It is not just emotional, but it comes from deep within our hearts and is based upon our personal experience with Jesus Christ. So, we acknowledge that we are privileged to be chosen as God's children.

Third, we need to enter into this privileged praise, a place of worship. This is as personal and private as worship can get; the pouring out of gratefulness to Jesus for the privilege of being in His family. In Psalm 100, David closes the psalm with an exciting picture of how our great God is above all gods. How great is His name; forever the same and with some special qualities! For the Lord is good; He will never leave you nor forsake you. The goodness of the Lord leads us to giving thanks unto our God. Only those who love God can personally understand His goodness. The sinners and unsaved people focus on doing wrong. How can God allow this? But, we as Christians thank God for Jesus and His grace. David says, "God's mercy endures forever." We are worthy servants because God does not issue us a sentence for prison. When people die in sin, they lose everything; their treasure and blessings. But for us, the faithful, we will come before Him in judgment and His truth will endure forever. Then, this is a good reason for us to shout for joy. We better know His word of truth. Because, His truth is our anchor and His word is our spiritual food. It will stand forever and is unchangeable.

This Thanksgiving, let's start to be more thankful to God for our blessings. Thanksgiving was meant for the family to unite together; not for cookies or cooking contests, but for thanksgiving. Let us be thankful or it will be a gobble day. So, let us be thankful unto God for delivering us from the oppressor who comes in many forms. Let us be thankful that God directed us to this church, today. Let us be thankful that God has been patient with us. Let's be thankful for Jesus Christ for His grace; because, it is by His grace that we are here united together in worship. So, let's approach Thanksgiving with a grateful, thankful heart and a confessing mouth and a willing spirit. Let us be filled with the fruits of His spirit: love, joy, peace, happiness, goodness, meekness, kindness, and faith. Let's take them home with us so we can have a great Thanksgiving in Jesus' name. Amen, church? Amen!

WORSHIP PLANNING HELPS #5

"In all these things we are more than conquerors through Him that loved us."
- Romans 8:37

WELCOME:

Blessed are all those who take refuge in God. There is no better refuge known than Jesus Christ. Let's worship, today, and place ourselves in God's kingdom and express our love and joy to one another. It is a blessing to have you here, today. Welcome!

INVOCATION:

Almighty God, who challenges your children to live a life which demands strict discipline. Grant us the strength to live our lives each day in full commitment to You that we may not allow ourselves to be weakened by inactivity in the Christian life. We pray in our Savior's name. Amen.

CALL TO WORSHIP:

L: The Christian life has been compared to a contest where we compete as well-disciplined children.

C: We know from experience that we cannot let up in the least bit with our Christian commitment or we fall far behind in our challenge to life.

L: We have promised to live our lives for Christ.

C: We trust in Him to be our source of strength that we may achieve the victory awaiting us!

L: When weakness threatens our Christian living, it is good for us to remind ourselves of these words recorded by the Apostle Paul, in Philippians 3:13-14:

C: "Brethren, I count not myself to have apprehended: but this one thing I do, forgetting those things which are behind, and reaching forth unto those things which are before, I press toward the mark for the prize of the high calling of God in Christ Jesus."

OFFERING PRAYER:

The eyes of God are upon those who obey Him, on those who trust in His everlasting love, to save them from harm and keep them alive. Father, by our tithes, we declare our faithfulness and reverence unto Thee. By giving to the church and to Your kingdom, we declare our commitment unto Thee. By the giving of our time and finances, we declare our trust in Your love to save us. Receive these gifts and tithes from our hearts. In Jesus' name. Amen.

PRAYER FOR THE FAMILY OF GOD:

Dear Heavenly Father,

We worship Thee as our faithful provider, the creator of life. We praise You because You bless us. We remember how Your only Son's life was in danger from birth and how You provided for Him. Your plan for His life was fulfilled on the cross. Your goal was to guide Him through this life and deliver Him to His kingdom. You do the same for us as we seek Your guidance in our lives. Your spirit is always ready to help us. Help us to focus more on our spiritual lives, daily, than on our physical lives. Remind us that we are spiritual beings, created to love and serve You through Your Son, Jesus Christ. Teach us to live for You. We pray You will deliver this world from the hands of the evil one. May nations, people and races no longer be burdened, but united in common love from Your Son, Jesus Christ. Amen.

SUGGESTED HYMNS:
"Higher Ground"
"He's Everything to Me"
"What a Friend We Have in Jesus"
"He is Lord"
"Victory in Jesus"

BENEDICTION:
May Your unfailing love rest upon us, O Lord, as we put our hope in You. Bless each one, here, with Your spirit throughout this coming week. Amen.

SERMON #5: MORE THAN CONQUERORS

I Chronicles 28:9 & 10; Romans 8
Christian Living

A friend of mine was in front of me going out of church, one Sunday. The preacher was standing by the door as he always does to shake hands. He grabbed my friend by the hand and pulled him aside. The pastor said to him, "You need to join the army of the Lord, son!" My friend replied, "I'm already in the army of the Lord, pastor." The pastor questioned, "How come I don't see you in church except on Thanksgiving and Christmas?" My friend looked around and whispered, "It's because I'm in the secret service."

Well, this Christian life we are living is not a secret service at all. We are going through contradictions and impossibilities through this Christian life. Why? Church, I would like to introduce you to the Armageddon. It is here, now, the last war before the Lord comes. "Behold, He will come as a thief in the night." We want to do what is good, but we easily fall into sin. We want to worship God, but we easily get mad with our brothers and sisters at home or in the church. Sometimes, we want to serve God, but on the other hand, we want to satisfy our desires. Not just because we are grown up, can we do what we want to do. We want to live in peace with others, but on the other hand, nobody better disagree. Sometimes, we want to be a good parent, spouse, brother or sister, but sometimes, what they don't know about you won't hurt them. You want to be spirit filled, but at the same time, one drink won't hurt. There's a daily struggle and battle. It's a conflict between two natures, good and evil.

Paul addresses this in his letter to the church in Rome. (Romans 8:7, 8) Paul, whose credentials are unquestionable, sits down and takes time to write to his Christian brothers and sisters. He tells them, "Even though I am an apostle of Jesus, I have a confession to make to you. Even though I love God and Jesus, and even though I am filled with the Holy Spirit and worship God through Jesus Christ, His Son; and even though I am encouraged by God's Word and love to sing praises to God, there is still a spiritual battle going on inside of me. It's a battle of doing right or wrong." He says that everyone will go through this problem. He is instructed by God to tell us how to handle this conflict.

Paul says there are three things about this conflict that we need to know. First, Paul says that these battles are for real. In chapter seven, Paul talks about this in length. He says we do the things that we are against and we don't do the things we are supposed to do. Paul struggled with this spiritual growth which is attacked by evil. He calls this attack 'fiery darts' that the enemy shoots at us, until we meet with our brothers and sisters in the church. Then, it would be like a charcoal getting close to the rest of the charcoals and starting the fire; getting stronger in the spirit, and then, standing against the wrong.

The old person wants to hold on to sin, while the new person wants to let go of the sin. In Colossians 3:9 & 10, Paul says, "Lie not one to another, seeing that you have put off the old person with his deeds, and put on the good and new person in you." In II Corinthians 5:17, Paul says, "If you are in Christ you are a new creation, old things are passed away, behold all things are made new." This takes time. It is a process. We are working towards perfection. Remember, when a sinner receives Jesus Christ in his or her heart, it takes a prayer to do this. Likewise, to be a saint takes a lifetime. The truth of the matter is this, when we accept Jesus into our hearts, we are saved, sanctified, and we start walking in the spirit or with the spirit in holiness, and we are filled with the Holy Spirit. But, we should act like it, even though we are still in the flesh.

We know that there is pleasure out there and a lot of sin. Paul tells us, in Ephesians 5:19, that we should read a scripture in the Bible, every day, to strengthen ourselves. Read a psalm; sing hymns and spiritual songs to God. Make melody in your hearts unto the Lord, giving thanks in all things to God. This is so we won't fall into sin. Because the old person is wrapped around the new flesh, the old person is fading away, little by little. Matthew 26:41, Jesus says, "Watch and pray that you enter not into temptation; for your spirit is willing but your flesh is weak." The old nature is getting weaker. When we were saved, the old person did not move out; he just moved over, and he is not going to give up easily. Sometimes, our thoughts and actions and words will disappoint us. But, we have to keep on pressing on to higher ground.

Secondly, Paul points out that this battle is edifying. Paul discovered spiritual growth through his battles. He found out that this Christian life is not lived only on Sundays, but all week long. He found out that he was carnal; he practiced things that he wasn't supposed to do. He found out that he was not fully controlled by himself. We are strong spiritually because God helps us with His spirit within us. This is why we flourish a little bit with spiritual arrogance. Paul says, in I Corinthians 11:31, that this is where we need to judge ourselves so we won't be judged by others. Sometimes, this means we can't see the sin in our self and this makes it hard to control our life. Paul says to the Corinthians, "When we are judged by the word, we won't be condemned with the world." Paul says that we are being renewed by the word, daily, because God loves us and the blood of His Son Jesus cleanses us from all sin. This battle within us helps the truth to be exposed. We might not see it right away, and people might not see it right away, but God does, and we ought to be thankful for our salvation; thankful to Him for leading us and guiding us away from sin, because we don't want to go back. We have come a long way to quit and go back. Satan would love to get us back to lying, gossiping, and sinning. He would love to reduce our participation in helping out in the Lord's service. But, we won't let Satan win this battle! We are more than conquerors through Him who died for us!

Thirdly, Paul says that we will be rewarded. Paul says that we will struggle, but there is a benefit. In Romans 8:19, Paul says, "The sufferings we go through cannot be compared to the treasures that will be revealed to us in heaven." We will know that we were not going through these battles alone. For one, the spirit will help us in our weakness; for when we get weak, then, the Holy Spirit comes to our aid and when we unite together in church, the sooner we will get help. The greater the struggle, the more powerful the Spirit will fall on us. The greater the struggle, the greater the treasure is, because "greater is He who is in us, then he who is in the world." The Spirit helps our infirmities. When we don't know what or how to pray, he makes intercession for us with groaning which cannot be uttered. (Romans 8:26)

The real battle is rewarding. We will struggle for a while and we might fall to our knees, but this is what Christians do; we get back up and say we are more than conquerors through him who purchased us. So, when we go through battles, remember to keep "forgetting what is behind and keep reaching for what is before you." Just say, "I'm pressing toward the mark for the prize for the treasure of the high calling in Jesus Christ."

There was a little girl who came from Bible study and sat with her family on the pew. She put her Bible down, and an older gentleman asked her if he could see her Bible. She replied, "You can look at it, but don't open it, because you'll let God out." Well, we would be better off if we would all open our Bibles and let God out. Amen, church? Amen.

"For God loves a cheerful giver." - II Corinthians 9:7

WELCOME:

Good morning! I am happy to welcome you to this morning's service. May it be a wonderful worship experience for everyone as we sing together praises to God.

INVOCATION:

Heavenly Father,

You have blessed us beyond measure and have given unto us all things freely. May our hearts be tuned to sing Your praise, and our hands be swift to do Your will, as servants of the Most High God. Amen.

CALL TO WORSHIP:

L: The earth is the Lord's and all who live in it.

C: He owns the cattle on a thousand hills, the wealth in every mine. He owns the rivers and the rocks and rills, the sun and stars that shine.

L: Whatever is good and perfect comes down to us from our Father who created all the lights in the heavens.

C: Wonderful riches more than tongue can tell. He is my Father. So, they are mine as well.

OFFERING PRAYER:

In Jesus' name, I pray for these offerings, O Lord, that they will help others hear about Your salvation and eternal life. May others come to know the joy of fellowship with Thee. I ask for a blessing upon these tithes. May they be returned back with a special blessing to those who gave joyfully. Amen.

PRAYER FOR THE FAMILY OF GOD:

In the name of Jesus Christ, we come to worship Thee, O God, who was, who is, and who shall ever be, and to sing praises to Your holy name. Your word is established forever in heaven, the only sure foundation in our lives. Thou art the one who calls us to life and sets us on a path that leads to joy. We bless Thee and give unto Thee thanks for all the ways in which Thou has given us signs of Your love. We thank You for those You have sent to be part of our lives, to direct us closer to Thee. We thank You for those who have served as disciples, placing Your reign before their own. We remember those who have taught us in Sunday school, our parents, those who have been like parents to us, pastors, and friends. We know Your steadfast love and trust never fails to care for those whom we carry In our hearts. We pray for those who are sick in body, in mind, and in spirit. We lift up those who have fallen astray, the hungry, and the homeless. We pray for those who grieve for their loved ones who have gone home. Bless them with peace, comfort, and strength. I pray for the congregation and their needs. Lord, manifest Your power in Jesus' name and bring healing to them. Let Your precious word be revealed through You Holy Spirit to accomplish that which we agree together in one accord, according to Thy word. Jesus said, "And He sent them the word and He healed them all that were there." And so it is that we come with faith because You send us Your word in spirit and in truth. We have the power and it is in the name of the Lord. Though Satan battles us, we shall not be defeated. Blessed be Your name, O Lord! Amen

SUGGESTED HYMNS:
"Great Is Thy Faithfulness"
"I Have Decided to Follow Jesus"
"Bringing in the Sheaves"
"In the Presence of Jehovah"
"In the Service of the King"
"Take My Life and Let It Be"

BENEDICTION:
Go and share the news that all may know the fullness of life through Jesus Christ. As we share this life, may our faith be strengthened through God's blessings, this coming week. In His name, Amen.

SERMON #6: GIVING OR NOT GIVING

Psalm 112; II Corinthians 8:6-15
Stewardship

The story is told of a pastor who phoned the home of some recent visitors to his church. A voice answered quietly, "Hello?" The pastor said, "Who is this?" There was a little whisper on the other end. "This is Jimmy." The pastor said, "How old are you, Jimmy?" "I'm four," Jimmy replied. "Jimmy, may I please speak to your mom?" "She's busy." Then, may I speak to your dad?" "He's busy, too." "Are there any other adults at your house?" "The police," Jimmy stated. "Well, could I speak to one of the police officers?" "They're all busy." "Who else is there?" "The firemen," Jimmy said. "Put one of the firemen on the phone." "They're busy." "Jimmy, what are they all doing?" "They're looking for me!"

Some Christians are just like little Jimmy. They are hiding out. This is especially true when it comes to people's responsibilities in the area of financial stewardship. Let's look at the exhortation on giving, found in II Corinthians 9:6-15. It concerns the needs of the believers in the church at Jerusalem.

Their region had a severe famine that had affected the city for more than ten years. So, the Apostle Paul led them in an effort to raise an offering for those believers who were going through this tragedy. The giving or not giving is seen by the Macedonian churches in the first part of this chapter. The churches in Philippi, Thessalonica, and Berea had outdone themselves in their giving to this need. Today, we want to reveal the giving or not giving seen in response to the church in Corinth.

There are three ways that people practice in this world. First, there are those who make things happen. Second, there are those who watch things happen. And third, there are those who don't even have a clue about what is happening!

The first point is potential; we have the power to withhold. The Corinthian church was a gifted church. They had the gifts of the Spirit in operation. But, something was missing. While they were a gifted church, they were not a generous church. Other areas of service are not to be a substitute for a lack of giving. Giving one's time to the church does not take the place of giving one's finances. Giving one's good support does not substitute for giving financially to your church. The Corinthians didn't need some authorized law from the apostle; they needed to prove their love by giving. Love is not selfish, but ready to help others. Love is not something you say. It is something you put into practice.

Word had been given out by the apostles about the need of the saints in Jerusalem. The Macedonia churches stepped in and got involved in this giving opportunity. The Corinthians church stood around and probably, at their monthly business meeting, talked about it, but decided they ought to pray about it first, before they did something. It is amazing that some churches allow a few members to hold them back from doing God's work and giving generously to help meet the need.

The second point is promise; keep your promises. If you have ever promised God you would tithe and give offerings, God has heard your prayer and expects you to keep it. A year before Paul had preached to them, when some were holding back their pledge. (I Corinthians 16:2) Some others were quick to help with this need. Paul had instructed them to give and put it into practice. Start with what you have. God will never give you more until you give from what you already have.

Once, a preacher came to see a farmer and asked him, "If you had $200, would you give $50 of it to the Lord?" The farmer proudly said, "I would." The preacher went on, "If you had two cows, would you give one of them to the Lord?" "Sure," the farmer answered. "If you had two pigs, would you give one of them to the Lord?" The farmer said, "Now, preacher, that is not fair. You know I have two pigs."

It takes no faith to give when you have extra. It is like saying, "When the harvest comes in, I will plant the seed. When the building is completed, I will buy the land." Giving is on the front end, not the back end. In Deuteronomy 28:13, Moses said, "And the Lord shall make thee the head and not the tail." It is an act of faith on our part and an act of obedience. It shows how weak the faith is when we are reluctant to give. The procedures that are followed in some churches remind me of Wall Street in New York City, instead of the dusty road in Jerusalem. The pressure of planning and fund raising and a lot of mailings may not be all wrong, but they are a lot of work even though there are blessings in them.

The equal opportunity mentioned here is not the amount, but the extent. The fact was that the Corinthians were blessed. And yet, some of them used a Bblical excuse to not give. "We are no longer under the law. We are under grace, and we don't have to tithe." True, we are not under the law. We live by grace and practice mercy. A wolf does not have mercy, but a lamb does. So, we give out of knowledge, obedience, and love; all of which is taught both in the Old Testament and in the New Testament. We do not fall under the statement that Hosea 4:6 states, "My people are destroyed because of lack of knowledge."

Let me ask a question this morning: How can we give less – under grace or under the law? Some people make excuses by saying, "Giving doesn't make sense to me." What is missing from the common sense most people have when it comes to tithing? It's God! They have left God out of their calculation and their worship. God told me that we are going to receive every single cent back on every tithe and offering we give plus ten percent for doing our part. And yet, others still use financial excuses like "I already have financial problems, and you say I need to give. I can't afford to give." It's just like saying, "A good aim is not good if you don't pull the trigger when you are out hunting." The truth is that people can't afford NOT to give. "If I had more, I would give, but, I can't afford to give." "There is no way that ninety percent after tithing is more than one hundred percent without tithing." "I give my time to God, so I am not responsible to give my money." "I give to various other causes, so I don't have to give so much to the church." Some people give other excuses for not giving.

There are differences between us in our financial abilities. But, look at your life. You have a decent job, a few nice benefits, a retirement plan, a house, food, clothes, and a car. Some people would love to trade places with you for one day; to work just one day at your job for your pay. Some have many excuses. But, we have every reason in this world to give, because "Jesus will never send us anywhere He has not gone, to face anything He has not faced, to love anyone He has not loved, or to give anything He has not given."

I would like to share a humorous illustration this morning. There was a church that didn't have the reputation for being very generous with their giving. The pastor thought it was time to do something drastic in order to teach the congregation the importance of giving. He contracted an electrician and had all of the pews wired. The next Sunday which was the first Sunday of the New Year, the time when the church had traditionally taken up pledges from the people, the pastor stood up and made this announcement, "From now on, instead of putting your pledges in sealed envelopes and turning them into the church office, all pledges will be made publicly during the worship service. So, let's get started. All of you, who will pledge to give ten dollars a week, please stand up." As soon as he said this, he pushed a button that the electrician had installed in the pulpit and it sent a light shock of electricity through the wire and into the pews. Immediately, half of the congregation jumped to their feet. The pastor then said, "Praise the Lord! Now, please follow the ushers to the back for further instructions." Then, he reached down and turned the knob on the podium a little bit higher and said to the rest of the people, "All of you, who will pledge to give twenty dollars a week, please stand." He pushed the button and the current of electricity caused several people to rise to their feet. "Praise the Lord!" said the pastor. The ushers had to work twice as hard just to record all the names and pledges. After the service, the pastor and his staff were busy adding up the totals on their extremely successful annual stewardship drive until one of the elders came in from the sanctuary and ended their enthusiasm by announcing, "Only four church members were electrocuted because they refused to stand up."

Well, if we give according to God's word, He guarantees us much more than we could ever store up. And our test results are found in Luke 6:38,"Give and it shall be given unto you, good measure, pressed down, and shaken together running over, shall people give into your bosom; for the same measure that you give with, it shall be measured back to you again. So, lay your treasures up where moth and dust do not corrupt." Give God your best and He will take care of the rest in your life. So, let's work together as good stewards unto the Lord and in our ministry for Him. To God be all the glory now and forever. Amen!

"Behold, I send my messenger before thy face, which shall prepare thy way before thee."
— Matthew 10:10

WELCOME:
We welcome you today as we gather for this time of worship and reflection on God's love. May God inspire you and bless your hearts and lives, today.

INVOCATION:
God whose word is forever established in heaven,
Engrave Your words onto our hearts so we might become Your children through the power of Your Holy Spirit. Let Your word, which is sweeter than honey and more to be desired than gold, shine through our lives revealing through our brokenness Your perfect love for all people. Amen.

CALL TO WORSHIP:
L: The law of the Lord is perfect, reviving the soul; the decrees of the Lord are sure, making wise the simple;
C: The precepts of the Lord are right, rejoicing the heart; the commandment of the Lord is clear, enlightening the eyes;
L: The fear of the Lord is pure, enduring forever; the ordinances of the Lord are true and righteous altogether.
ALL: More to be desired are they than gold, even much fine gold; sweeter also than honey and drippings of the honeycomb.

OFFERING PRAYER:
Father,
In the name of Jesus, we present these gifts unto Thee as we offer our love and obedience to Thy word. We love you. May these gifts be used to care for others. Amen.

PRAYER FOR THE FAMILY OF GOD:
In the mighty name of Jesus Christ, we come humbly before Your beautiful throne of grace. Lord, Your wisdom is beyond our comprehension. We look at this creation and are surprised by the simple things. There is greatness in creation that is too powerful to comprehend. We bless Your beautiful name and give You thanks for all the blessings we have received from Thee. We thank You for the way our minds work and think and feel. We thank You for the way our brains can adjust and learn. We thank You for the vision that You give us toward the truly important things of life. You reveal to us how we can live life to its fullest. You dwell within us and around us so that we can become what we are with power in us. We thank You for a time as this to be here together to worship Thee. With care You have created this world,

and so, we know that You care for us. We pray for those who are in distress and pain, today, Lord. Send Your precious spirit and soothe them and heal them in Jesus' name. We stand on Your word and we claim Your promises to meet our every need. Amen.

SUGGESTED HYMNS:
"Standing on the Promises"
"How Firm a Foundation"
"Wonderful Words of Life"
"Thy Word is a Lamp"
"Gentle Shepherd"
"Where He Leads Me"
"Softly and Tenderly"

BENEDICTION:
May the Lord protect you and bless you. May the love of God be with you in your home. May every breath of air you take, strengthen you and fill you with rest. May the word of God keep your soul, body, and spirit watered and fed with good fruit from God's harvest until we meet again in church. Amen.

SERMON #7: GOD HAS THE LAST WORD

Malachi 3:1-5; Matthew 11:10-15
Advent

When we open our Bibles, God is calling us to do our part by opening our hearts to the Word of God. God will open our eyes and that will open our minds to His word. When we open the Bible, the first five books are the Law of Moses: Genesis, Exodus, Leviticus, Numbers, and Deuteronomy. Then, we have the history books of the Bible which are twelve books: Joshua, Judges, Ruth, I and II Samuel, I and II Kings, I and II Chronicles, Ezra, Nehemiah, and Esther. Next, we have the five poetry books of Job, Psalms, Proverbs, Ecclesiastes, and Song of Solomon. These are toward the middle of the Bible, and they are good wisdom books to read and meditate on in the mornings or any time. And then, we come to the last seventeen books of prophecy. Now these are divided into five Major Prophets: Isaiah, Jeremiah, Lamentations, Daniel, and Ezekiel. These are excellent prophecy books to read. Next come twelve minor prophet books which are small, but powerful even to the dividing of the soul and spirit: Hosea, Joel, Amos, Obadiah, Jonah, Micah, Nahum, Habakkuk, Zephaniah, Haggai, Zechariah, and Malachi.

Malachi is the last Old Testament minor prophet. Malachi is a Hebrew name meaning "my messenger". Scholars say that it may be regarded as an abbreviation of Malakhiyah. This prophet should have been placed with the Major Prophets because of the prophecy of John the Baptist and the Messiah and the closing of the Old Testament. It has the largest Bible study in the world. Yet, it is one of the smallest books in the Bible.

Malachi was a young priest. The author, Ezra, wrote this book during the Persian domination of Israel, around 444 B. C. Before this, Zechariah had encouraged the people to remodel Solomon's temple for God. But, the priests were polluting the temple. So, God sent His prophet, Malachi, to preach to them. The Israelites would yell out, "Who is this guy, preaching to Israel about God's love? Rebuking Israel's unfaithfulness? Rebuking our priests? Preaching the need of tithing and the day of judgment? Who is this young man?" He is the minor prophet called Malachiyah!

This miniature book is a summary of the entire Old Testament and briefly covers five keys of truth found in the entire Old Testament: first, Israel is chosen by God; second, The transgression of Israel against God; third, the manifestation of the Messiah and the name of God; fourth, the manifestation of the tribulation upon the nations; and fifth, the purification of the people in the church.

Malachi can be compared with Moses' first book of the Law in Old Testament, Genesis. Moses gave the first Old Testament prophecy concerning the Messiah (Genesis 3:15) while Malachi gives the last Old Testament prophecy concerning the Messiah (Malachi 4:2). Malachi comes preaching, announcing the coming of John the Baptist. As God's continuing messenger, he will be the next voice preaching after Malachi. But, God has the last word! Do you know what it is like to have the last word? Having the last word means that nobody has anything to say to top your words. In the family, fathers usually have the last word.

But, there was a young boy who had the last word. A little boy was standing on the sidewalk in the middle of a city block. He was obviously waiting for something. An older man approached him and asked, "Who are you waiting for?" The little boy confidently told the older man that he was waiting for the bus. "Oh," the man laughed, "the bus stop is in the next block." The boy insisted that the bus was going to pick him up right where he was at. The older man became annoyed at what he thought was disrespect. He raised his voice and told the little boy that he'd better start walking if he hoped to ride that bus. The boy replied politely that he would wait for the bus right there where he stood. The man frowned at the little boy and started walking off. But then, he heard screeching brakes. He turned around to see what was happening, and to his surprise, he couldn't believe his eyes. The bus was actually stopping for that little boy. The bus door opened and the boy started climbing aboard. But, just before he went in, he turned to the old man and yelled, "Hey, Mister! My daddy is the bus driver."

And so it was with Israel, God had the last word through the prophet, Malachi. One thing we do know is that Malachi concentrates on the future. So, we ought to concentrate on the future, too. Malachi pours out the whole message of the Old Testament in this small book of four chapters; the messages of faith, love, and hope – Messiah's coming. Hosanna in the highest! Blessed are they who come in the name of the Lord. Gladly shall they enter into the kingdom of heaven; for He shall come riding on a mule, bearing the name of the most high God. It's this same hope that gives unity to all the books in the Old Testament. And it is this same hope that gives us unity, because Malachi's message is written for the entire Bible. There is hope, church! There is hope coming.

Prophets were walking down the fields, proclaiming the message of hope. And now, it is here, the name of God is here; Jesus! Some denominations need to go back and re-read the whole Old Testament, again. There is a lot to learn about Jesus, the Messiah.

Malachi closes the stormy period of Israel's exile and distress with a flare of light that flames in the darkness. Every follower of His word came to add new fuel to the message with expectancy. You just have to concentrate on Jesus being right next to you, sitting by a table or on His throne, when you pray to Him. It will start burning in your heart as your faith starts working in you. Malachi comes with a sweeping hand, casting fresh fuel on the flames. Faith causes it to leap even higher and closer to God and brighter than ever before. Malachi's words are the words of a forerunner, a prophet. "Behold, I will send my messenger to prepare the way of the Lord! Blessed are they who come in the name of the Lord." Isaiah heard this same voice in a prophetic vision, back in 850 B. C.; the voice of a forerunner, John the Baptist. If we want a prayer answered, we have to prepare the way and make straight our pathway. "Seek, knock, ask, and it shall be given unto you." It is important to know that Malachi wasn't calculating time here. He is making a definite announcement of a fact. The next prophet in Israel will herald the coming of the Lord! How did he know this? Well, for us, the answer is simple; God sent Him.

Now, Malachi makes it definite that this judge will judge them, but with love for their good works. But, everyone who makes it into heaven will come before God and Jesus for their judgment. Israel knew that the prophets would preach, "Repent for Jehovah will judge you for your disobedience; an eye for an eye and a tooth for a tooth." But, this Messiah, He is a good, gentle Shepherd who will live in your hearts. In Matthew 10:33, Jesus says, "Whosoever shall deny me before people, him will I deny before my Father which is in heaven." We better stick to that name, Jesus, because it has salvation. Jehovah means creator. We have been created already. Now, we need salvation and Jesus means salvation. Amen!

Matthew 12:30 says, "He that is not with Me is against Me, he that gathers not with Me, scatters abroad." We will be blessed if we follow Jesus Christ. I John 4:4 says, "Greater is He that is in us than he that is in the world." And this is the message; Jesus came and sacrificed His life for us so that we will surrender and sacrifice our life for Him. Jesus doesn't own us until we have Him in our hearts.

There was a business store owner, cleaning the outside windows. When he came across a spot, he wiped it with Windex, over and over again. Then, he decided to try it through the inside. Sure enough, it came off. The problem was on the inside. Sounds like us. We try to remove the stains from our past with tears and pain. We rub and rub, but the stain is in the inside. Nothing can clean it, but the blood of Jesus Christ. Apply it by using the mighty hand of the Holy Spirit.

The four hundred years between Malachi and John the Baptist have long come and gone, ending the Old Testament. "And behold, the curtain of the altar was torn in two from the top to the bottom." Now, the New Testament scriptures say, "The Word has become flesh, and now dwells with us, and we see His glory, the glory of the only begotten Son of God." (John 1:14)

Will we let God have the last word in our lives? Will we let Him cleanse us from all sin and strife? Will we let Him purify our mind, body, soul, and spirit? One of the ways we do this is by coming together in church and hearing His word and putting it into practice. "Faith comes by hearing, and hearing by the word of God." (Romans 10:17) "But without faith it is impossible to please God, for he that comes must believe that He is a rewarder of them that diligently seek Him." (Hebrews 11:6) So, let's remember Malachi's message of hope for tomorrow. What we do, today, depends on how we are going to live tomorrow. Let's receive God's word this morning. I can hear the Master calling, "Will you receive My friendship? Will you receive My glory? Will you receive My love? Will you receive your freedom? Will you receive forgiveness and healing? Will you receive action for reaction and extraordinary for the ordinary? I want to hear a loud yes, three times. Yes! Yes! Yes! Father, Son, and Holy Spirit! In Jesus' name, be blessed. Amen!

"And I John saw the holy city, New Jerusalem, coming down from God out of heaven."
- Revelation 21:2

WELCOME:

Good morning! We extend a warm welcome to all who have come to worship. May we be encouraged and inspired to live as people who are pressing on toward our heavenly home where we will live forever in the presence of God.

INVOCATION:

Heavenly Father,

You have called us to be Your own and adopted us as Your sons and daughters. Enter into our midst and be praised by Your children. Grant us a new awareness of the heavenly home you are preparing for us, and teach us to ever praise You. Amen.

CALL TO WORSHIP:

L: We come together today as strangers and pilgrims on this earth.

C: This world is not our home. We are looking for a better place, a heavenly place.

L: We are looking for a city whose builder and maker is God.

C: We are looking for a holy city where God dwells.

L: With eyes of faith, we can see God's eternal home as a reality.

C: How lovely is Thy dwelling place, O Lord! Blessed are those who dwell in Your house. They are ever praising You!

OFFERING PRAYER:

God, the gifts of our pockets and purses are of no value if we have not first given You our hearts and offered You our lives. Our money is worthless in Your eyes if it is not accompanied by obedience to all of Your word. God who searches our hearts and knows each one of us, inside and out, may these offerings be pleasing and acceptable to You and be used for Your kingdom. Amen.

PRAYER FOR THE FAMILY OF GOD:

Dear God, in Jesus' name, we come before You. You have been our help in time of need. We confess that often we do not have much hope for years to come. As we read and watch the news, our faith fails. We wonder about the world's future and our own future. We forget about Your promises along with Your great saving acts in Your word. We thank You, most patient God, for keeping faith with us in spite of our doubt, and for providing for us in time of need. And now, Lord, we are gathered together this morning. We thank You for permitting us to fellowship together and to worship You in spirit and in truth. Yet, we know that Christianity was never meant to be lived in isolation. Let us take to heart the importance of this fellowship in Your sight. Help us to work and pray to build up Your house, for we are one in Your sight and cannot stand before You as private individuals only. We ask You for good health for this congregation. Let love abound in it and bless us with strength to continue this week. Give us a spirit of devotion to Your people and move us to cleave to one another in times of gladness and affliction. Help us, also, to be genuinely welcoming to those whom You would join to us in the future. We thank You also for those saints who have come before us to this place, who built this building and furnished it, who put the hymn books in the pews, and even remembered the congregation in their wills. Let us not take for granted all the hopes and care so many have poured into this congregation. Bend our hearts, O Lord, to love Your church and to love You with all our hearts, souls, and strength, and minds. In Jesus' mighty name, let Your will be done on earth as it is in heaven. Amen.

SUGGESTED HYMNS:
"This World Is Not My Home"
"Sweet By and By"
"Holy Ground"
"In the Presence of Jehovah"
"Mansion Over the Hilltop"
"When We All Get to Heaven"

BENEDICTION:
Go and share the fruit of the Spirit with love, joy, peace, patience, kindness, generosity, faithfulness, gentleness, and self-control with your friends and family. May God keep His eyes upon you, this week, as you walk boldly towards the New Jerusalem. Amen

SERMON #8: THE NEW JERUSALEM

Psalm 84; Revelation 21:1-27
Prophecy

We are only given a glimpse of heaven as John describes a vivid portrait of the New Jerusalem. It is found in the book of Revelation. The writer is John, Jesus' younger step brother, who had already written four books in the New Testament: the Gospel of John, I John, II John, and III John. He was blessed to reach farther into eternity than any other author in the whole Bible. Revelation is the only prophetical book in the New Testament, and is similar to seventeen books written in the Old Testament. Revelation is the only book in the entire Bible which begins by promising a blessing on those who read it and study it; and it ends with a curse on those who add or take away from it.

Now, let's look at some of the differences between Genesis and Revelation. In the beginning, in Genesis 1:10, God divides the waters which He called the seas. In Revelation 21:1, God does away with the waters called the seas and there is no more sea. In Genesis 1:27, it describes Adam with his wife, Eve, in the Garden of Eden, reigning over the earth. In Revelation 21:9, it describes the last Adam with His wife, which is the church of God, in the New Jerusalem. In Genesis 1:5-16, God created the sun and the moon for the day and the night. In Revelation 21:23, the city has no need of the sun, neither of the moon, to shine in it; for the glory of God gives it light, and the Lamb is the light thereof. In Genesis 3:22, the tree of life is denied to sinful people. In Revelation 22:2, the tree of life gives its fruit, every month, and the leaves are for the healing of the people. In Genesis 3:17, God says, "Cursed is the ground for your sake." But, in Revelation 22:3, God says, "And there shall be no more curses for you." In Genesis 3:1, Satan appears to torment people in the world. In Revelation 20:10, Satan disappears to be tormented forever in the lake of fire. In Genesis 7:12, the earth was punished through a flood during the time of Noah. But, in II Peter 3:7, the new earth shall be purified through a fire in the day of judgment. In Genesis 2:10, a river went out of Eden to water the garden and it was parted in four ways, for the people always lived by a river. In Revelation 22:1, people will live close to a river. "And He showed me a pure river of water of life, clear as crystal, proceeding out of the throne of God and of the Lamb. In Genesis 23:2, the patriarch, Abraham, goes to weep for Sarah. In Revelation 21:4, the children of Abraham will have Jireh their Provider wipe away all tears from their eyes. In Genesis 19, God destroys the earthly twin cities, wicked Sodom and Gomorrah, from the desert sands. In Revelation 21:1, God presents a new heavenly city, the New Jerusalem, coming out of heaven. Genesis 50:1-3 ends with a believer in Egypt, Jacob, stepping into eternity when he died. Revelation 21:4 ends with all believers in eternity, reigning forever, some in the New Jerusalem and some in the new mansion Jesus promises us.

The New Jerusalem is not made by the hands of man, but created by Jehovah God, descending like a beautiful bride adorned for her husband. Everyone is going to see it. This is not going to be like Sodom and Gomorrah which tempted people toward evil desires of possession and pleasure. This is a clean New Jerusalem whose habitation is Jeshua who visits with His own people. No sin or evil shall ever separate us from God. No physical barriers of sea and sky. No more emotional fears and no more separations. God and His people are finally going to be together.

The Father had not revealed His name in the Old Testament, but in the New Testament, His name was revealed to us in His Son, Jesus. In II Corinthians 5:17, we read, "Therefore, if anyone is in Jesus Christ, they are a new creation; old things are passed away; behold all things are made new." No more littering in the market place. No more widowed mothers, no more riots or wars, and no more pulling one another down. Behold all things are made new. This New Jerusalem is fitting to house the Alpha and the Omega, the Beginning and the End. This New Jerusalem signifies the beginning of our inheritance and the end of our struggles, the beginning of peace and the end of all kinds of wars. It is a city to whom all are attracted, but few will make it in. Only the faithful shall be allowed to come in and take up residence and to keep up the New Jerusalem. And as strange as it may be, we shall worship faithfully with the Holy Spirit, the Son and the Father, in a new manner for they will be present there. This is a glowing city, a brightly adorned and dressed up city that will attract even the sinner who shall desire to take up residence, but it could be too late as the New Jerusalem comes down out of heaven adorned beautifully.

When I was younger and a Catholic, I prayed to the Virgin Mary, every day for one year. As I completed that year, Mary came to visit me twice, on that last day and on the following day, in two dreams. She told me that I was not supposed to worship her, but her Son Jesus, the Savior of the world. She was dressed beautifully. She said, "This is the way we dress here, it's not my fault. Tell the people to worship my Son Jesus." Every time she spoke a word, it made me feel a joy unspeakable.

In the New Jerusalem, kings and people shall be drawn to its promise of peaceful habitation, but the wicked shall be turned away and forbidden to enter in. The word of God says, "But the fearful and the unbelieving and the abominable, and murderers, all liars, and adulterers, fornicators, witchcraft and idol worshippers, all these shall be cast out into the lake of fire which burns with brimstone." (Revelation 21:8)

Heaven and the New Jerusalem are real. They are a refreshing place, a relief place, a restricted place, a place of riches, a place of relationships, and a place of remaining. Paul says, "For our conversation is in heaven; from whence also we look for the Savior, the Lord Jesus Christ." (Philippians 3:20). The New Jerusalem challenges us to come up higher. So why then do people live in the valley of sin and bondage when Jesus and heaven is being shared with them? Why do they suffer in torment when joy is only a confession away? "For the conversion of a sinner takes only a moment, but the growth of a saint takes a lifetime." A sinful tongue is full of poison and it will ruin our praise and worship unto God. So, let's prepare and get on board to the city of God, the New Jerusalem adorned as for her husband. According to Revelation 20 and 21, this old heaven and earth will be destroyed. The word of God says, in Matthew 24:39, "Heaven and earth shall pass away, but My words shall not pass away." II Peter 3:10 says, "But the day of the Lord will come as a thief in the night, in which the heaven shall pass away with a loud noise, and the elements shall melt with a fervent heat; the earth also and the works that are therein shall be burned up. The New Jerusalem is pictured, when this happens, as a stationary city floating above the earth in the sky. According to our measurements, this city would be roughly 1,500 miles long, wide, and high. If placed in America, it would reach from New York City to Denver, Colorado or from Canada to Florida. It has twelve gates made of pearl and an angel guards each gate, and they will remain open forever. It shines with the beautiful colors of jasper clear crystal, sapphire blue, greenish blue, royal blue, apple green, emerald green, beryl green, yellowish green, yellow quartz, topaz yellow-white with brown streaks, deep red, and purple. There are many different colored vines and vegetables, fruit trees, animals, and people, the continuation of the clear crystal river of life with beautiful waterfalls and fountains. The colors coming from the temple of the Lord shine blue for deity, white for purity, and purple for royalty.

There was a little girl, born blind, who would ask her mom about the different colors of the world; the flowers, the trees, the snow, and the ocean. But, the little girl could only imagine. At ten years old, she had an experimental surgery done to help her see. She had the bandages on for weeks until the time came to take them off. She ran to the window and stood there breathless. "Mother," she said, "why didn't you tell me it was so beautiful?" "I tried, Honey, but words aren't enough."

I believe that in heaven, we will look around breathless; and when we see the Apostle John, we will say to him, "Why didn't you tell me it was so beautiful?" And he will say, "I tried, but words aren't enough!" Paul says, In I Corinthians 2:9, "But as it is written, eye hath not seen, nor ear heard, neither have entered into the heart of people, the things which God has prepared for them that love Him." Church, let's grow a deeper love for God and expect lots of love, peace, joy, happiness, meekness, gentleness, goodness, faith, and riches when we are called to heaven and to the New Jerusalem. Amen.

WORSHIP PLANNING HELPS #9

"If you will confess with your mouth the Lord Jesus, and believe in your heart that God raised Him from the dead, you will be saved." - Romans 10:9

WELCOME:
Welcome to all who have come to worship. May our time together in God's presence ignite our faith with the resolve to share the message of salvation.

INVOCATION:
Loving Father,
We worship You, the One who brings salvation through Jesus Christ. Thank You for the gift of redemption. As Jesus gave His all for us, let us commit ourselves to giving our all for Him, in whose name we pray. Amen.

CALL TO WORSHIP:
L: Throughout time, when confronted with the salvation of God, man has responded, "What must I do to be saved?"
C: And the answer resounds, "Believe in the Lord Jesus Christ and you will be saved."
L: Today, we ask, "What does it mean to believe, Lord?"
C: And the answer burns in our hearts, "Take up your cross and follow Me."
L: If we believe that Jesus can save us from our sins, we will not ignore God's commands. We must believe to the point of obedience.
C: This, we truly believe, Lord. Help our unbelief.

OFFERING PRAYER:
We offer unto Thee, O Lord, these gifts that Thou hast blessed us with. We open ourselves to You and Your converting love. So, strengthen our faith that we may be instruments in converting the world for Your kingdom. Amen.

PRAYER FOR THE FAMILY OF GOD:
In the precious name above all names, Jesus Christ, we come before Thee, Almighty God. We worship Thee, O God, because Thou art all knowing. There is nothing hidden from Thee. You have created us in Your own image and have given us the ability to know ourselves. For You know us better than we know ourselves. You invite us to look within and face the truth of our own lives. We thank You for taking care of us, this past week, and for the blessings, too. Lord, please forgive those who have sinned against You and have not yet asked for forgiveness. For You have promised to forgive us and cleanse us from all unrighteousness. We bring to You the cares of our hearts, not because You need to be told, but because we need to tell You. We need to share with You, our loving God, the deepest concerns of our own lives. We need to bring the hurts of the world to You so we can stand with You in Your word, caring for the

hurting and the lost. Heal them, O Lord, for Your kingdom for they belong to You. May You be glorified in us, O Lord. Amen.

SUGGESTED HYMNS:
"I Believe in a Hill Called Mt. Calvary"
"I Know Whom I Have Believed"
"At the Cross"
"Open Our Eyes, Lord"
"I Surrender All"

BENEDICTION:
May the Lord bless you and keep you. May the Lord make His face to shine on you, and be gracious to you. May He lift you up and give you peace, strength, and love, this week. Amen.

SERMON #9: HAVE YOU BEEN CONVERTED?

Acts 26:9-32; John 16:1-3
Evangelism

The Apostle Paul was converted by a heavenly vision. It was the vision and the word of Jesus that changed his whole life. It was an awesome revelation that converted his life from a persecutor to a Christian to a preacher of the gospel. Before his conversion, he persecuted the church and everyone serving Jesus. So, the people had to come up with another name. They called Jesus the Christ meaning the 'anointed one'. Remember the Greek word Christian; Christ plus tian means 'Christ servant' or Christian. Paul's inhumanity toward the Christians was known throughout the area. People were afraid of Saul of Tarsus. Saul persecuted the Christians and burned at the post some of them. He would order his soldiers to pluck their eyes out with a burning stick in order for them to denounce the name above all names, Jesus. And some denominations are still looking for other names to serve Him by! Well, all the Christians were praying for help and the Lord heard their prayers. One day, Paul met the Lord of lords, King of kings on the road to Damascus. With the authority and commission from the chief priest to stop Christianity by all means, Saul was on his way to persecute the Christians in Damascus. You see Saul was a Pharisee and had influence with the chief priest. As Saul was traveling with some of the soldiers through the Damascus road, he met a very powerful force that threw him and his soldiers off their horses. It was a light from heaven. The Lord Jesus Christ appeared in the light and started to convert Saul of Tarsus through this heavenly vision. The soldiers could see a light from heaven surrounding all of them. They felt the power and the radiance that was flowing out from Saul's body. They, too, were shocked. It wasn't at night. It wasn't in a house. It wasn't in a synagogue. No, it was in the middle of the day, out in an open field. I can imagine what they were thinking, "What great light is this that shines before us brighter than the sun?"

In some incidents in the Old Testament, God spoke and manifested himself in the thick darkness. The scripture says, "He spoke to Abraham in the great dispensation of darkness." But now, the light and the life eternal have been brought to us by the word of Jesus. Jesus appeared in a great light. When some people die, the first thing they feel is that radiant light that awakens them, and they see Jesus standing right in front of them with an outstretched hand, saying, "Come unto Me all ye who are tired and weary, and I will give you rest." (Matthew 11:28)

Jesus is the light of the world. The soldiers who traveled with Saul saw the light only; they didn't hear the voice, much less see Jesus. Why? Because, many are called but few are chosen. (Matthew 20:16) Paul heard the voice in the language of his own religion. "Saul, Saul, why persecuteth thou Me? It is awful for thee to kick and stab." "Who art Thou, Lord?" "I am Jesus, whom thou persecuteth." The Lord told Saul, "Stand upon your feet, for I have appeared unto thee in a vision for a purpose, to make you an instrument of the gospel." The Lord told Saul to preach to the Jews and the Gentiles that their eyes may be opened; that they may turn from darkness unto the light of the gospel, that they may turn from the power of Satan unto the power of God, that they may receive forgiveness of sin for eternal life. He spoke these same words of salvation to King Agrippa and the Governor Festus. He told them, "You have to obey this heavenly vision." Paul preached the suffering death and the burial and resurrection of Jesus Christ. He spoke of how Jesus was the first one to rise from the dead, and how He would shine His light among both the Jews and Gentiles. Paul had so much faith in Jesus, that Governor Festus said with a loud voice, "Saul, you have gone crazy! Much studying makes you mad. Just yesterday, you were persecuting the servants of Jesus." "And now, Governor, I have seen the light, the glorious gospel light. I am not mad, most honorable Festus. I speak the truth. King Agrippa, you believe the prophets. I know you do!" The words of Paul inspired the king. Then, the king stood up and the governor and Bernice and they that sat with them and the king looked around and said, "Saul, you almost persuaded me to become a Christian." You could have heard a pin drop. Everyone was silent.

In Acts 11:26, it says, "And the disciples were first called Christians in Antioch." Now, what is the value of almost being converted? I am glad you want to know, because there is no value in almost being converted. "Almost" will not give you any security. Almost being a Christian is not enough. God created you; He did not make anything half created, much less half Christian. You are either a Christian or not. We cannot be walking on two roads at the same time. We either have to walk on the narrow road to heaven or the wide road to hell. We must have both feet on the road we choose. Jesus said, "Strait is the gate and narrow is the way which leads to life, and few will there be that find it." (Matthew 7:14)

When the Lord called us out of darkness into His marvelous light, He called us all the way. God is calling people, every day, for divine salvation and deliverance. He can bless you with a vision like He did Saul. He could speak to us by visions and dreams as he did with Isaac and Abraham. He could speak to us like He did with Samuel. And Samuel replied, "Here am I, Lord, speak with that soft voice." God can send us a messenger like He did with David and Hezekiah. He could send us a messenger with a message as he did with Daniel and Zacharias and the Virgin Mary. God can call us to His service by an internal voice as He did with Jeremiah and Ezekiel. God can speak to us as He did with Isaiah. And Isaiah replied, "Lord, woe is me for I am a man of unclean lips and I dwell with an unclean people. For mine eyes have seen the Lord, high and mighty. And the smoke that came out as He was walking filled the temple." (Isaiah 6:1-5) Jeshuah spoke to Israel in visions. God spoke to Jacob in visions and dreams. God blessed Hosea with the gift to prophesy with visions. God spoke to Joseph in dreams and visions, too. Then, Jesus openly spoke with the apostles.

But there are reasons why God does not speak to everyone in visions and dreams. Some people do not rely on dreams while others do not rely on visions. But, we can rely on His holy word. We can come to church and earn a diamond, every time, under our heavenly name! If the law of the Lord is in our hearts, then, none of our steps will slide; because "He is the way, the truth, and the life, and nobody comes unto the Father except through Jesus Christ." (John 14:6)

Our true conversion gives us a vision of faith to worship our Lord Jesus. Our conversion offers submission to His kingdom and declares our dependence on Him. Our conversion confronts our sin and seeks His forgiveness and sets our relationships in order. Our conversion looks for Jesus and follows Him. It provides the key to a rich spiritual life and an intimate relationship with Jesus. Our conversion gives us the right to release the anointing God has placed in our lives to bless our fields, to bless our future, to bless our wealth, and to bless our family with the power of the Holy Spirit in Jesus Christ. "For we delight ourselves in the Lord and He will give us the desires of our hearts."

Church, keep your faith vision strong for we are moved by Noah's faith to build an ark. But, many were washed away by the flood because they were almost converted. Lot's wife escaped the fire and brimstone as it destroyed the twin cities of Sodom and Gomorrah, but she was almost converted and she looked back and was turned into a pillar of salt. Pharaoh was almost converted by setting the Israelites free from bondage, but he and the Egyptian Army planned to bring them back and were drowned in the Red Sea. We cannot be blessed by almost loving our enemy. We have to do what is good to them. Luke 6:27 says, "But, I say unto you who can hear, love your enemies, do good to them which hate you. For great is your reward." Yes, it is bigger than we can think of. And we cannot be blessed by almost forgiving someone who wronged us. We have to forgive them or we will pay the consequences. We have to believe Matthew 6:15, "If you forgive not men their trespasses, neither will your heavenly Father forgive your trespasses." We cannot be blessed by almost giving our tithes. We have to tithe our ten percent. We cannot go to heaven by almost being saved. We have to accept Jesus and be redeemed by the blood of the Lamb, sanctified by the spirit of God, and cleansed by the word, if we want to make it into heaven.

Jesus said that He would come back for a church without spot, blemish, or wrinkles. (Revelation 3:15, 16) And now, let me ask you; "Have you been converted to serve God with all your heart?" If you are almost converted, then, come to Jesus. He said, "Behold, today is the day of salvation." (II Corinthians 6:2)

"As often as you eat this bread and drink this cup, you remember my death."
- I Corinthians 11:26

WELCOME:

The Lord be with you. We gather, today, to remember. We remember the institution of the Lord's Supper. We remember the Lord Jesus as He suffered and died for our sins. We remember the unity that is ours in Christ Jesus, and we remember the salvation that God gave us because of His mercy and His loving kindness toward us.

INVOCATION:

Heavenly Father,

We come into Your holy presence to worship You for the gift of salvation. We come to remember Your love and sacrifice that redeems us from all unrighteousness. We come to open our hearts to Your searching and Your cleansing. May Your love and mercy renew in us a right spirit and a clean heart. Amen.

CALL TO WORSHIP:

L: Grace unto you and peace from God, who was and who is and who is to come.
C: And from Jesus Christ, the faithful witness, the first born of the dead, ruler above all rulers of the earth.
L: I love Jesus who suffered death to free us from our sins.
C: Making all who confess Christ a nation of priests set apart for God's service.
ALL: To Jesus Christ be glory and power forever and ever! Amen.

OFFERING PRAYER:

Dear Father God, in Jesus name, we come unto Thee, with our tithes and offerings. Use these gifts for the work of the church's ministries of reconciliation and mercy. Amen

PRAYER FOR THE FAMILY OF GOD:

O Most Holy God, we thank You for creating us along with the universe we live in, and for placing us here on earth to serve You. We thank You for making us into You own image and giving us a mind to search for You and a heart to love You. Thank You for providing for all our needs, physically and spiritually. Above all, we thank You for sending Your Son to be our Lord and a Friend who sticks closer than a brother. For our salvation, we are thankful to You, far beyond the power of words. Around this table, spread Your presence like You did with the apostles. We have gathered once again to celebrate Jesus' life. We remember His humble birth and His youthful wisdom, His obedience to His family, His devotion to His disciples and His compassion for all of them. We remember His teachings and His calm in crisis, His generosity toward His enemies. We remember His sorrow and His courage before His judges, His forgiveness toward His executioners and the victory with which You rewarded Him by raising Him from the dead on the third day. We pray now for Your spirit to empower us in the celebration of the sacrament of His presence. Let this bread and this juice from the vine become for us reminders of His broken body and shed blood. If we are asked, "Were you there when they crucified my Lord?" Let us answer, "Yes, we were there, and we were of no more use than the disciples." So, let us approach His table that we may experience His mercy and His love. Amen.

SUGGESTED HYMNS:
"Family of God"
"Sweet, Sweet Spirit"
"The Old Rugged Cross"
"Cleanse Me"
"When I Survey the Wondrous Cross"
"Bind Us Together"

BENEDICTION:
Eternal Lord, as we leave this place of worship and communion, may we know that You never leave us nor forsake us. Help us to go with faith in our hearts, the peace of Jesus in our lives, the protection of the spirit beside us, and the security of Your presence in us, this week. Amen.

SERMON #10: DO THIS IN REMEMBRANCE OF ME

Matthew 26:26-30
Communion

What is "Do this in remembrance of Me" all about? Do we fully understand what this Lord's Supper, we participate in, is supposed to mean? Or, do we just take the Lord's Supper because that is what a Christian does in church?

I read, this week, about a small church in New York City. They had the same pastor in the church for thirty five years. Every time, they had the Lord's Supper, the pastor would get static electricity on his hands. So, before he handed out the elements, he would go by the radiator and touch it to release the static so he would not shock the people. He made this his custom through the long years of serving in the church. When he retired, he was replaced by a young pastor. This church was the pastor's first church, and in the first month, they participated in the Lord's Supper. But, he didn't get any static electricity like the other pastor had. He didn't even think about the radiator. To his surprise, he was in trouble because he didn't touch the radiator like the other pastor. He called one of the lay leaders of the church and asked if something was wrong. "Well, pastor, yes. It's the way you did the communion service. You see, our pastor, before he distributed the communion elements, would go and touch the radiator." "Touch the radiator?" asked the young pastor. "I never heard of that tradition before." So, the young pastor called the former pastor and asked him if he would touch the radiator every time he would distribute the elements for communion. "Oh, yes, I did, always, to discharge the static electricity so I wouldn't shock the people." The congregation thought that touching the radiator was part of the holy tradition.

The truth is that we as God's people find ourselves doing things just because we have always done them that way. Well, I want to look into God's Word and see what it has to say about "Do this in remembrance of Me" and discover why we do it.

An account of the meal that Jesus celebrated with His disciples can be found in Matthew 26. Jesus was alone with the twelve disciples, in the upper room, to celebrate the Passover. The Old Testament Passover was one of the oldest Jewish traditions. It came before the priesthood and the Law and it was commanded by God when Israel was in Egypt. Now, Jesus was about to teach the disciples that this Passover meal was going to change. This was going to be the last meal that they would have together, and Jesus wanted them to know they didn't have to sacrifice animals for the forgiveness of sins. He was about to do away with the animal sacrifices in the Old Testament covenant and give them the Lord's Supper of the New Testament covenant. What we see is an old covenant transforming into a new covenant. Jesus wanted the people to see a new way for this celebration meal. .

Jesus had been teaching and preaching the gospel, and people were hearing it. People were beginning to follow Him; some for the wrong reasons. They saw Jesus as a wise and gifted teacher who could multiply food and heal the sick. The Scribes and Pharisees saw Him as a troublemaker who was trying to make them look bad. But, He was winning the hearts of the people who were listening to His word. Soon, He was going to pay the price for sin by shedding His own blood on the cross and He wanted to leave a remembrance to celebrate the freedom from slavery to an eternal relationship with Jesus

So, Jesus took some bread and offered a blessing of thanksgiving to His Heavenly Father. This is an example for us as we bless our food when we eat. Jesus broke the bread before He gave it to His disciples and commanded them to take and eat. The fact that He broke the bread did not symbolize a broken body. John made it clear that in fulfillment of prophecy "not a bone of Him shall be broken." (John 19:36) The same was true of the Passover lamb that was sacrificed. Not a single bone of that lamb was broken. (Exodus 12:46) So, the bread represents the body of Jesus sacrificed for us. Jesus gave it an entirely new meaning saying, "This is my body which is given for you." It represents a separation from sin and the beginning of holiness and godliness by His divine authority.

And the same thing was involved with drinking the cup. Jesus took the cup and gave thanks commanding, "Drink from it all of you." As the disciples drank from the cup, Jesus said, "This is my blood of the new covenant." (Luke 22:20) The cup represents the blood of Jesus shed for us. When Jesus brought reconciliation, the price was the shedding of blood because without shedding of blood, there is no remission for sin. (Hebrews 9:22) Jesus did not simply have to die, but had to shed His blood. (I Peter 1:2) He shed His blood from the wounds of the crown of thorns, from the scourging, and from the nail holes in His hands and feet. After He was dead, a great deal of His blood poured out from the stabbing spear thrust into His side. His death made the relationship with God possible. The blood made the forgiveness of sins for all people; Gentiles as well as Jews who will trust in the Lord.

These two acts of Jesus are normal features of "Do this in remembrance of Me."; unleavened bread and the grape juice are the Lord's Supper for all Christians. (I Corinthians 11:27-29) We can see the elements for what they truly are; the symbols of Jesus' body and blood given to us to know God.

It is very important to have a proper attitude to participate in this meal. In I Corinthians 11:27, Paul says that to participate in an unworthy manner is sin against the Lord. People will get sick. Paul says, "Examine your hearts before you partake of this meal." The only people who are allowed to partake of the bread and the grape juice are those who are willing to stop sinning and confess Jesus Christ to others. We have to practice this breaking of bread and drinking of the juice and examining our hearts.

The Lord's Supper is a remembrance as well as a commandment. The Lord's Supper is a new remembrance of redemption that the Lord will honor forever. For the disciples, the Lord's Supper began in the upper room. For us, it should begin in the church. Jesus said that He would not drink of the fruit of the vine with us, again, until that day when He would drink it new with us in His Father's kingdom. So, "Do this in remembrance of Jesus." Amen.

Printed in the United States
By Bookmasters